Once Was More Than Enough

by

Carl Kaplan

authorHOUSE®

AuthorHouse™
1663 Liberty Drive, Suite 200
Bloomington, IN 47403
www.authorhouse.com
Phone: 1-800-839-8640

First published by AuthorHouse 4/15/2008

ISBN: 978-1-4343-5891-2 (sc)

Printed in the United States of America
Bloomington, Indiana

This book is printed on acid-free paper.

...And they said I couldn't replicate myself. Actually, I was told to "go replicate yourself" by many readers.

My first collection, "Bottom of the Barrel" turned out to be a runway success. That was no typographical error. It was discovered that by tying six books together a perfect airplane wheel chock was created. Thank you, Delta.

This work is a companion piece to "Bottom" and both are intended to be read together (more sales). I have graduated to limericks, moving up a rung or two on the writing depth chart. Stephen Sondheim wants to be remembered for his music; I want to be known for the words.

I'm told this book, similar to the recent release by Mr. Greenspan will be "embargoed". Mine, however, will be at the request of the reading public. As the plumbers say, "Thank God for leaks".

Enjoy!

Carl Kaplan

Dedication

To My Grandaughter

Emery Pearl is a grandad's delight
Won't let her out of my sight
With her twinkling eyes
And her wistful sighs
I love her with all of my might.

"Modern Adoption" magazine gives one free issue for every subscription.

Teachers of printing techniques impart a fontain of knowledge.

When Calvin Klein's lawyer died he was buried in briefs.

A person who trounced attacker with champagne bottle acted with brut force.

Perambulating phlebologists block the nations' arteries.

Offended generals took umbrage in a fierce battle.

Love struck librarians have dewey eyes.

Meat cutting moil favors a brisket (which is also the name of his tool box).

What was the rallying cry of the California peasants' revolution?
Surfs up!!!

Carl Kaplan

Saddam's brother lost his head over the revolution.

Saddam's brother was well hung.*

*Hung well may be better form but it is a local ethnic restaurant.

Saddam's brother always wanted to behead of state.

Saddam Hussein almost got away but he fell into a trap.

Work clothes tailors do overall overhaul.

Eminent domainers took shelter in a quick court fight.

At the start of a vocabulary contest they play the national antonym.

Jewish wives give great headache.

It takes a fortune to explore undersea which is why Jacques Costeau so much.

Successful neurologists' business card: I Give Great Head; I Don't Take Assignment.

Defaulting dermatologists have blemishes on their records.

Irate furnace salesmen post heated messages.

Skeptical naval enlistees are not impressed.

An Army OB/GYN is in the cervix of our country.

When comparisons are inapt, things aren't what they simile.

If the Mustang Ranch amended its financial results it would be a restatement of tarts.

A poet's immediate popularity produced a metaphoric rise to fame.

All Thai people have a Siamese connection.

The head meteorologist is the raining expert in the field.

Accused otolaryngologists deserve a hearing.

Carl Kaplan

The King's book on the Roundtable made him a published arthur.

TV host's suicide note: "I won't be back after this message."*

_____

* Merv Griffin stole this from me. He said the above words would be on his tombstone.

Short sleeve purple shirts are always in style; the right to bear arms is inviolate.

The first female urologist: Urethra Franklin.

The first female anesthesiologist: Urether Franklin.

The first female Xmas ornament designer: Urwreatha Franklin.

Carl Kaplan

Midnight internet messages are nocturnal emissions.

Rhyming jurists mete out poetic justice.

Movie making moils have final cut.

Once the cheese course is served, a meal is feta accompli.

Singing psychiatrists counsel their patients with shrink rap.

Canonical nudity: a naked nun and a defrocked priest.

Where did spinning start? Sakhelin Islands.

A space alien, landing in a German music school, asked a student: "Take me to your lieder".

Carl Kaplan

Jewish prostitutes are happy hoeckers.

Carl Kaplan

It was difficult to schedule Heather Mills and Sen. Dole on "Dancing With The Stars"; it cost ABC an arm and a leg.

A letter carrier in Salt Lake City is a Mormon mailer.

Orthodontists get paid by the visit, but they prefer to be on retainer.

A Jewish Cuban hit man is a Havana Killa.

Perverted Italian chefs have foot fettucines.

Podiatrist's wedding vows: "Toe Death Do Us Part".

"Mums" the word at Tehran's annual anti-semantic games.

When a lawyer's office is closed they put up a "No Soliciting" sign.

The confidential memo from the senior management of Depends was never sent – there was a leak.

Podiatrists are devoted to their patients; they just don't walk away.

He who rummages through the bread basket leaves no scone unturned.

Carl Kaplan

Best selling authors are prose.

An artist's color sense are pigments of his imagination.

A CSI's prayer: Someday my prints will come.

In Paris, the asylum is on Rue Mania
In Bucharest, the asylum is in RueMania

The national anthem in Helsinki: it's not how you start, it's how you…..

He who pees in sleep suffers from urinary unconsciousness.

Deceased listing brokers are viewed in open houses.

In medieval times noblemen played the lute; lawyers played the lyre.

Henry VIII was measured at 12", after all, he was a ruler.

The police lost the tree bandit in a copse.

The film on incontinence was cancelled when the writer goofed on the script: the actors didn't have a plot to piss in.

Singing dentists are gum rappers.

The Dutch version of a large passenger vehicle is a VanGo.

A baby pig in Denmark is a hamlet.

A money order in Taiwan is a Shanghai check.

Carl Kaplan

The robber barons' good works were gilt trips.

Parkinson sufferers buy Shaker furniture.

Orthodontists work in pairs
So that they can brace their patients.

Maligning orthopedists cast aspersions.

Free podiatry clinics foot the bill.

Ceylonese buyers go on shopping sris.

The end of an opera about the Mafia is called a coda of silence.

Sheep herder's lament on loss of his herd: there will never be another ewe.

A rabbit fetus is an ingrown hare.

Drink The White Stuff

A milk truck gets to pass all the cars
Because it has
The white of whey

In The Garden

The cook asked the spices who put oregano in the sauce.
Rosemary and sage refused to say, but thyme named the perp.
See only thyme would tell.

Fungus You

Who's there among us
Not 'fraid of a fungus
That grows night and day
In every which way
Until it becomes humongous

Mushroom

Our hero was from Portobello
A strapping and muscular fellow
When drafted to fight
He fainted from fright
Turned out Portobello was yellow.

Brittany as Well

Dollars to donuts
Lindsay Lohan will go nuts
She'll begin seeing bugs
They'll give her the drugs
And she'll sleepily say bon nottes.

Rated X - I

A blow job is very delicious
To do it was once meritricious
But Bill Clinton Pres-ex
Says it's really not sex
And Monica's claim: it's nutritious.

Rated X - II

There once was a man in Helsinki
Who was cursed with a long erect blinki
Ashamed by the pole
To the surgeons he stole
And was fitted with a malleable slinki.

Rated X - III

Massages on the deck
To help my aching neck
And as she probed down low
The blood began to flow
And I went from wreck to erec.....

Rated X - IV

Julius Caesar, no political hack
For ruling Rome he had a knack
Citizens were known to hear
That Julie was queer
Cause he took one in the …. (back)

Rated X - V

Viagra, Cialis and such
Will get you hard very much
For erections of 6 months or more
Call Ripley's or maybe a whore
For viewing or perhaps a touch.

Rated X - VI

There once was a Lady from Chelm
  Who did it for coins of the realm.
  When trouble did find her,
  Her men stood behind her
They loved it when she took the helm.

Rated X - VII

<u>Films Featured in the First Viagra Film Festival:</u>

"Pecker"
"Mopy Dick"
"Standing Tall"
"Peniles from Heaven"
"Coming Home"
"Inching Up"
"Size Counts"
"Oozing Members"
"44 Magnum"
"The Erection of the Hesparus"
"Don't Be Too Hard On Yourself"
"Throw Me a High Hard One"
"What's Up Doc"
"If I'm Not Ready, Start Without Me"

Above Politics - I

I watched the movie "Waitress"
I found myself in distress
Adultery is good, abortion is bad
Smoking is good, it's ever so sad
That the heroine becomes her MD's mistress.

Above Politics - II

Abortion should be
A right that is free
No need for a hanger
No bleeding in anger
It's her choice
As to whether to be.

Below Politics

Rickover was one of his friends
For which Jimmy C made no amends
He went right off the track
He failed in Iraq
His problem was he had the bends.

Politics - I

There is a chance Chaney is dead
Electrodes implanted in his head
So if we pull his plug
With just a quick tug
We might have no Chaney to dread.

Politics - II

We appeal to the chief
We show him our grief
A dead daughter, a dead son
With a war that can't be won
But government's just a bit deef.

Politics - III

Mayor Bloomberg's money clip
Could buy him speech or quip
Could he run out in front
Will he lead or just grunt
Depends on the writers' pentip.

Politics - IV

The President seems to be thinking
That he can govern simply by winking
The soldiers they die
We all weep a sigh
The President sure must be drinking.

Politics - V

Gonzalez, Rumsfeld & Chaney
A combination so zany
Respected before
They broke the law
Their defense – we're a little insane-y.

Poliltics - VI

Hillary's running away
Her vote lead may be here to stay
If a Veep she could find
She'd leave no lead behind
Oh, remember that the time is only May.

Politics - VII

The Republicans don't seem to care
That defeat flies in the air
Let the dollar implode
The exports unload
No wonder a surplus is rare.

Politics - VIII

In an act of dementus
Bush commuted his sentence
Libby did the crime
He should do the time
Then we might consider his repentence

Politics - IX

In the midst of the Iraq war mania
Where most think we are insania
Our younguns are dying
The government's lying
And the President –
He goes to Albania.

Politics - X

Wolfowitz said he blamed the press
For raking up much of the mess
His girlfriend said" Honey
I need much more money
As she wriggled out of her dress.

WWII Scoreboard

Who won the war?
Fight from Tokyo to Azore
A Mercedes here
A Toyota there
We allowed the axis to soar.

Productivity

The farmer was singing the blues
His cow was not taking his cues
He turned to a cow mutterer
A word, then udder butterer
The mutterer became the cow's moo-se.

Royalty's Perks

It was great to be the Tsar
Subjects came from near and far
To see his fountain's flow
To add up all his dough
And he knew there was no one on his par.

TB Guy

The guy's in isolation
But is that any consolation
To the many he has passed
Maybe coughed or maybe gassed
"Are we sick?" they ask with rapt anticipation.

TB or Not

He dreamed up a plot while in rem:
People scared he'd be coughing on them
TB guy will be a star
The film bound to go far
'Case it's the first to focus on phlegm.

Feeling Better - I

The positive power of prayer
Brings moments of joy that are rare
So make sure you savor
Those feelings you favor
And blot out your thoughts of despair

Feeling Better - II

The release of endorphin
Allows you to morph-in
To the person of your dreams
And better than it seems
You might just wind up thin.

Above Religion

God told Noah it would poura
That was written in the Torah
Noah said poor is me
The animals go for free
So he called the Ark "The Schnorrer".

Hopes

For today's class the subject is war
The best way to make it no more.
With prayer and some guidance
We can leave it behind us
And then hope our spirits will soar.

Do It Yourself

A key to success is opinion
The difference between losing and winion
So keep being first in your mind
And you'll be out of the bind
That separates the great from the minion.

Animal Rites

Dogs are a blessing for you
Keep you happy and not blue
They stay at your feet
Your heart drops a beat
So get one without further adieu.

Hamptons - 2007

Bridgehampton is crowded this Summer
To get from here to there is a bummer
From east end to west
27 is best
But to cross it you will need a Hummer.

Medical Miracles

Botox makes you smooth
It keeps you in your groove
No wrinkles or regret
Who cares how old you get
You even might hang in the Louvre.

Yankee Stadium – May '07

The Yankees are having a season
Which could defy rhyming or reason
The hitters don't hit
The pitching is sh*t
At this point we hope they've been teasin'.

Early May – Yankee Stadium 2007

The Yankees traded for A-Rod
So the crowds they could yell Hooray-Rod
To homers and doubles
The end of their troubles
Instead he hits like a Nay-Rod.

Yankee Stadium - Again

If I were Jason Giami
Now walking around like a zombi
My foot in a cast
How long will it last
I'd bet these events were beyond me.

U.N. Visit

The Iranian came to the city
He thought he was quite witty
The Holocaust was not
Israel could go rot
That he's here is such a pity.

Vatican Follies

Poles and Germans
Make good Popes
and fulfill the world's high hopes
If in matters of preaching
They might need teaching
They have the Italians
To show them the ropes

Ira_

The Iman he was a fretter
That the Iran/Iraq war was not better
No one got the noose
Too bad 'twas a truce
'Cause the winner would change but one letter.

Our Ally

The Muslim guy from Saud
Preached very much and so loud
Throw the infidels out -
He had that much clout
That we died in a vast mushroom cloud.

Indian Giver

An upstart chap from Delhi
Strove with fire in his belly
Enticed to err legal
He was penned with a Siegel
So all that he could do was watch telly.

Security Line

Packing for a trip
The mind does a little flip
What liquid does qualify
How about makeup for my eye
I fret as my plastic bag goes zip.

Vacation - I

Computer unrest in Estonia
Boy-that's a bunch of baloney-a
They just have one board
If you cut the cord
It might bring on anhedonia.

Vacation - II

In Finland it was cold and damp
We need vodka to light our lamp
Walked and shopped but mostly drank
Finnish vodka of imperial rank
And on return crawled up the ramp

Vacation - III

Stockholm for its size
Offers shoppers many buys
While browsing in the marts
Bought a box with six neat parts
Now I own the prized Piece Prize.

Vacation - IV

In Denmark we went to a hostel
To try to save some cost-el
On spotting our Vuitton
And our clothing soon neat on
The group at the hostel went hostile.

Vacation - V

Walking in Warnemunde
Seemed like a perfect blunder
But the beach was sublime
And we discovered a mime
Warnemunde, what funde.

Vacation - VI

The cruise ship docked in Tallin
Where gas costs $10 per gallon
The city was fine
We drank some fine wine
But on balance I'd rather just sail on.

Carl Kaplan

Vacation - VII

Our tour is almost done
But the final stop was fun
The sunshine abounded
The denizens grounded
The day was a total homeRunne.

Vacation - VIII

It is raining so much in Geneva
I've taken to bed with a fever
The lake is real fine
And so is the wine
But the weather is my pet peev-er.

Vacation - IX

On days when the cruising is endless
The good part is that you will spend less
No bus tours, no shopping
You're free of bar hopping
And the relaxation will be mindless

Vacation - X

The table was set for sea views
The dinner finale dé cruise
Our twelve days were fun rare
Our glasses lift for one prayer
That the friendships we made we won't lose.

Vacation - XI

Summing up the cruise:
We saw unbelievable views
In Norway we saw fiords
We even went to Lourdes
And then again in Paris 'twas the rues.

Fabulous French

The French are an interesting group
Their ways throw us for a loop
From oeuvre to oeuf
Or by being aloof
Only they can turn merde into poop.

Just Desserts

The contents of the Hermitage
Send us a simple messiage
The Tsar said its all mine
You serfs don't cross the line
And that's why Nick had no safe passiage.

Spare Time

A trivia game is perplexing
The queries externally vexing
We strive hard to solve
There's no want of resolve
But the topics are way to complexing.

Keep Your Mouth Shut

Messed with the King – called him a liar
Wound up on the funeral pyre
Made a mistake with the ruler
Who couldn't be crueler
He thought as the fire grew higher.

On the West Side Subway

If you miss the B
You wait for the C
Time goes by interminable
Palpitations discernable
For this they charge you a fee.

Law and Order - I

The city's cops are a-shooting
they love the root-toot-a-tooting
Unarmed perps
The cops think they're twerps
So they plug them
Whether or not they are looting.

Law and Order - II

Three thugs with an uzi
Gunned a cop on a Tuesday
The crooks were then caught
The cop died – in short
The trio will get theirs on nooseday.

Ode To A Photographer

The photos of Bill Ray are grand
His print work is in great demand
From shutter to negative
So many years in consecutive
By this time he's become a brand.

Aging

Remember the fame?
Remember your name?
Will it all come back?
Did your memory crack?
Old age: loopy and lame.

End of the Show

The Sopranos are quite near the end
Tony's enemy could be his friend
If one of the pack
Goes behind Tony's back
The gangsters could all wind up penned.

Old Guys' Reunion

Many years they have passed
Since we're seen our classmates last
50 years is awesome
We all aged and then some
But we're still going to have a blast.

Going, Going…..

I have no fear
Al fin is near
My life was fine
No regrets are mine
So goodbye dear.

CPSIA information can be obtained at www.ICGtesting.com
Printed in the USA
LVOW08s0709130614

389810LV00001BA/169/P